Earthquake!

by Cynthia Pratt Nicolson

Kids Can Press

**This book is dedicated to my mother-in-law, Bernice Nicolson,
and to the memory of my father-in-law, Don Nicolson**

Acknowledgments

My thanks to Bob Turner, a research scientist with the Geological Survey of Canada, for reading the draft manuscript for this book. Bob's love of nature in all its guises and his enthusiasm for generously sharing his knowledge are an inspiration.

Once again, it's been great to work with the crew at Kids Can Press. Stacey Roderick and Val Wyatt edited the manuscript with care and insight, Patricia Buckley tracked down some incredible photos, Julia Naimska gave the book its lively format and Bill Slavin lightened a serious topic with his drawings. Thanks to them all!

Kids Can Press acknowledges the financial support of the Ontario Arts Council, the Canada Council for the Arts and the Government of Canada, through the BPIDP, for our publishing activity.

Published in Canada by	Published in the U.S. by
Kids Can Press Ltd.	Kids Can Press Ltd.
29 Birch Avenue	2250 Military Road
Toronto, ON M4V 1E2	Tonawanda, NY 14150

www.kidscanpress.com

Edited by Val Wyatt and Stacey Roderick
Designed by Julia Naimska
Printed and bound in Hong Kong by Book Art Inc., Toronto

The hardcover edition of this book is smyth sewn casebound.
The paperback edition of this book is limp sewn with a drawn-on cover.

CM 02 0 9 8 7 6 5 4 3 2 1
CM PA 02 0 9 8 7 6 5 4 3 2 1

National Library of Canada Cataloguing in Publication Data

Nicolson, Cynthia Pratt
   Earthquake!

(Disaster)
Includes index.

ISBN 1-55074-949-8 (bound)   ISBN 1-55074-968-4 (pbk.)

1. Earthquakes — Juvenile literature. I. Title. II. Series: Disaster (Toronto, Ont.)

QE521.3.N5322 2001   j551.22   C2001-900828-7

Kids Can Press is a Nelvana company

CONTENTS

EARTHQUAKE Jolts City!

Early in the morning of January 17, 1995, the Japanese city of Kobe was rocked by a powerful earthquake. The quake jerked sleeping people out of their beds. It felt like a nightmare — but its terrors were real.

In the darkness, screams rang out as people stumbled from their damaged houses and crumbled apartment buildings. Dust and smoke filled the air. Sirens wailed as emergency crews raced to the worst-hit areas.

A car lies crushed under heavy clay roof tiles in Kobe, Japan, after a major earthquake hit the city in 1995. Many older homes collapsed because the weight of traditional tile roofs was too great for their shaking walls.

A section of the massive Hanshin Expressway toppled when the magnitude 6.9 earthquake shook Kobe. Engineers from Japan and other countries studied the collapsed structure. By figuring out what went wrong, they hope to improve bridge and highway design in the future.

The earthquake broke gas pipes and knocked down electrical wires. Fires blazed where sparks from fallen wires ignited leaking gas. Firefighters couldn't control the flames because of broken water pipes and piles of rubble that blocked their way.

While some neighborhoods suffered little damage, other streets were destroyed.

Thousands of buildings collapsed during the earthquake. About 4500 people died and 35 000 more were injured when roofs and walls fell on them or fire consumed their homes. Most of the city's 1.5 million residents were safe, but shocked. As the day dawned, they gazed in horror at their ravaged city.

Surrounded by devastation, survivors of the Kobe earthquake struggle to save a few precious possessions. About 180 000 buildings were destroyed by the earthquake and the fires it set off. But many modern buildings, such as those in the background of this photo, withstood the quake with little or no damage.

Dealing with DESTRUCTION

A man wheels his bicycle past ruined buildings on a Kobe street. After the earthquake, residents had to walk or cycle everywhere because roads were clogged with debris, and trains and buses weren't running. Dangerously damaged buildings, such as those shown here, were later flattened by demolition crews to make room for new construction.

Over 200 000 people were suddenly made homeless by the 1995 earthquake in Kobe, Japan. Hundreds of families moved away immediately. Others stayed to rebuild their city, and their lives.

Many people gathered in schools and churches. Others camped outside, shivering in the damp winter weather. With no electricity, the homeless residents were forced to cook over small fires. They lined up in the streets to receive food and bottled water.

Crews worked frantically to restore the city's services. Within five days, most parts of the city had electricity. Water pipes took longer to fix. Finally, on March 31, Kobe once again had drinking water.

DISASTER DATA

Our planet quivers with thousands of earthquakes every day. Most are gentle jiggles, too small to be felt. Others vibrate the ground — like a bus or truck passing by. Each year, a few big quakes knock down buildings and bridges. These giant jolts can also cause landslides, floods and huge ocean waves called tsunamis.

Although people can't stop earthquakes, they *can* learn how to prepare for them. Around the world, seismologists (scientists who study earthquakes) are working with engineers and emergency planners to keep people safe when the ground begins to shake.

But nothing could restore the lives lost during the quake. Although it tossed Kobe for only twenty seconds, the earthquake's effects would be felt for years.

Earthquake survivors use emergency telephones to contact worried friends and relatives. Some people had to wait several days before finding out that their families or friends in Kobe were safe.

Our Sizzling PLANET

Have you ever dug a hole? If so, you probably noticed that the ground is cool just below the surface. If you could dig to the center of the Earth, however, you would be in for a surprise. Deep inside, our planet is scorching hot.

Earth's seething core has two parts — an outer core of liquid metals and a solid inner core. Two other layers — the mantle and the crust — surround the core. The mantle is a thick layer of hot, semi-solid rock. The crust is the cool, rocky surface we walk on every day.

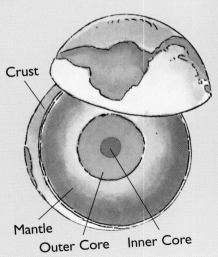

Crust

Mantle

Outer Core   Inner Core

Every 65 minutes, the Old Faithful geyser in Yellowstone National Park shoots out searing jets of steam. Hot water from deep in Earth's crust rises into an underground chamber. Pressure builds and builds until the super-hot water explodes upward in a spray of water and steam.

Although it seems solid under our feet, Earth's crust is broken into about twenty chunks called tectonic plates. The plates float like giant rafts on the softer rock of the mantle. Pulled by currents in the mantle, they glide apart, scrape together and smash head-on. All this action causes major changes. Mountains rise, volcanoes erupt and earthquakes shake the ground!

In 1912, scientist Alfred Wegener (left) published his theory that the continents are moving. At the time, many people thought he was crazy. This 1930 photo shows Wegener with an Inuit guide on an expedition in Greenland. Wegener died just a few weeks later.

Mid-winter bathers enjoy the hot springs of Banff in the Canadian Rockies. Hot springs form when heated water seeps up through cracks in Earth's crust and becomes trapped in rocky pools.

You Try It

Use a hard-boiled egg to make a mini-model of Earth. Gently tap the egg on a table to crack the shell all over. Then ask an adult to slice the egg carefully in half.

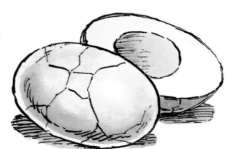

The cracked shell is like Earth's broken crust. The egg white and yolk are like our planet's mantle and core.

STRESSED OUT

Here's a little geology experiment. Hold out your hand and watch your fingernails grow. Pretty boring, huh? Your fingernails grow about 2.5 cm (1 in.) per year — the tectonic plates that make up Earth's crust move at about the same speed. But even though the plates drift so slowly, they pack a major wallop when they pull apart, collide or squeeze past one another.

The slow-motion dance of tectonic plates scrunches and twists the rock in Earth's crust. Incredible tension builds up as rock is squished in one direction or stretched in another. Like a twig that you bend, rock stores the stress — for a while. Eventually, the stress becomes too great. Just as the twig snaps, rock breaks, releasing the pent-up energy in a massive jolt called an earthquake.

A snakelike bend in railroad tracks shows how the ground moved during a 1976 quake in Guatemala. A fault (a crack in Earth's crust) crosses under the tracks where the people are standing. During the earthquake, land along the fault shifted sharply, breaking rock and moving the tracks more than 1 m (3 ft.).

Layers of rock have been tilted and twisted by the forceful motions of Earth's crust. Rock usually bends slowly and steadily under this pressure. Sometimes, however, it breaks suddenly, releasing waves of energy in an earthquake.

Rescue workers search for survivors in the tangled wreckage of an apartment building after a magnitude 7.6 earthquake in Taiwan. In this part of the world, the small Philippine plate slowly grinds into the large Eurasian plate. Sometimes, the two plates get stuck. When they suddenly jerk past each other, earthquakes shake the ground.

YOU TRY IT

To see how earthquakes happen, wrap sandpaper around two blocks of wood. Attach the sandpaper firmly with a hammer and nails. Press the blocks together, then try to slide one forward while you pull the other back.

Like rock on the edges of tectonic plates, the sandpaper keeps the blocks from sliding. When the force of your pushing becomes too strong, the blocks jerk past each other, just like the sudden movement of tectonic plates during an earthquake.

Where THE ACTION IS

Earthquakes can happen anywhere. But most often they shake the ground near the edges of tectonic plates. That's why parts of the world such as Japan, Turkey, Indonesia and the west coast of North America frequently feel tremors. Meanwhile, places far from the plate boundaries, including Australia and the central United States, are rarely shaken.

When Earth's plates suddenly shift along their boundaries, nearby places feel the shock. Moving plates usually trigger earthquakes in one of four ways.

• At some plate boundaries, such as the one off the coast of Japan, a seafloor plate dives under a lighter continental plate.

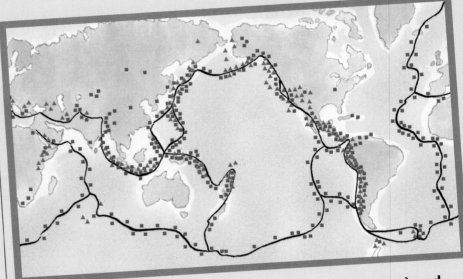

Most of the world's earthquakes (shown here as squares) and volcanoes (shown here as triangles) happen near the coasts of countries circling the Pacific Ocean. This sizzling, trembling loop is called the Ring of Fire. On this map, black lines outline the edges of Earth's tectonic plates.

• In other areas, plates collide head-on. In northern India and Tibet, colliding plates have created the Himalaya mountains and caused many earthquakes.

• Earthquakes also happen in places, such as East Africa, where two plates are pulling away from each other.

• In some spots, two plates slide past each other, heading in different directions. The Pacific plate, for instance, slips north along the North American plate at the San Andreas Fault in California.

A man strides past destroyed homes in western India after a magnitude 7.7 quake hit the area on January 27, 2001. The massive quake was caused by the collision of the Indian and Eurasian tectonic plates.

Clouds of steam rise from Mount St. Helens. It lies on the west coast of the United States, where the Juan de Fuca plate plunges under the North American plate, creating volcanoes and earthquakes.

DISASTER DATA

Earthquakes sometimes shake areas far from plate edges. New Madrid, Missouri, was rocked by three mega-quakes in 1811 and 1812. The shocks rang church bells in Boston and caused the Mississippi River to run backward for several hours.

RIPPLES OF RUIN

An earthquake begins when underground rock breaks suddenly. The jolt sends waves of energy, called seismic waves, in every direction — up, down and sideways. The spot where the rock breaks is called the earthquake's focus. The place directly above the focus, where the waves reach Earth's surface, is called the quake's epicenter.

Epicenter

Focus

Seismic waves lose their energy as they move away from the focus. An earthquake that rattles dishes in a city near the epicenter may pass unnoticed in a town farther away. Even so, the vibrations from a strong earthquake travel all the way through the Earth. They can be picked up by scientific instruments on the other side of the world.

A young cyclist turns a buckled sidewalk into a bike ramp in Northridge, California. The sidewalk bent upward when earthquake waves rippled through the area in 1994.

Seismic waves come in two main types: surface waves and body waves. Surface waves are shallow. They wiggle along the top of the ground, causing it to move from side to side or up and down. Body waves are much deeper. They speed right through the Earth's inner layers.

Body waves, in turn, are divided into two groups: primary (P) waves and secondary (S) waves. The difference is in how they travel.

Primary waves cause the ground to contract and expand in a moving sequence the way railroad cars might bump together along a train after a sudden stop. They travel quickly and can penetrate Earth's core. P waves are the first to reach a location.

Secondary waves travel with slower snakelike motions. They move through Earth's crust and mantle only and do not penetrate Earth's liquid core.

Broken gas lines fuel a fire where earthquake waves ripped open a Northridge street.

YOU TRY IT

Use a Slinky toy and a skipping rope to see the difference between primary and secondary body waves.

Stretch the Slinky on the floor and ask a friend to hold one end while you hold the other. Quickly push and pull on the end you're holding. A ripple of energy scrunches and stretches the

Slinky in the same way a primary wave compresses and expands the ground.

Now ask your friend to take the other end of a skipping rope. Shake your end up and down. The high and low points you see moving along the rope are similar to the troughs and peaks of a secondary wave.

Measuring A MONSTER

An earthquake shakes you from your sleep. How strong was the quake? Over the years, scientists have developed different scales for measuring an earthquake's power.

The Richter scale was invented in 1935 by seismologists Charles Richter and Beno Gutenberg. It assesses the strength of an earthquake according to the height of the wiggles it produces on a seismogram (a record of the ground vibrations caused by an earthquake).

But the Richter scale doesn't work for really large quakes.

So, in 1978, Hiroo Kanamori and Thomas Hanks came up with a new scale. This measurement, called moment magnitude, is based on the total energy released in an earthquake. Each whole-number increase means a quake releases about thirty-two times more energy. A magnitude 6.2 quake, for example, is thirty-two times more energetic than a magnitude 5.2 quake.

In addition to an earthquake's magnitude, scientists measure the degree of damage it causes in a particular place. This is called an earthquake's intensity. The first intensity scale was

Books tumbled from the shelves of this Los Gatos, California, bookstore when an earthquake struck in 1989. Seismologists measure a quake's intensity by observing the damage it causes. Weak shaking, for instance, tosses a few cans from a grocery store's shelves. Strong shaking will topple the shelves, or even the store itself.

invented by Italian scientist Giuseppe Mercalli in 1902. It was later changed to become the Modified Mercalli Intensity Scale, which is still used today.

The Modified Mercalli Intensity Scale ranks earthquake intensity using twelve levels, labeled with Roman numerals or whole numbers.

A level I (1) quake causes shaking that people don't notice.

Level IV (4) feels as if a heavy truck has hit a building. It makes dishes rattle. Wooden walls creak and parked cars rock.

A level VII (7) quake makes it difficult to stand up. Plaster and brick fall from walls. Waves toss on ponds. Large bells ring.

At level X (10), most brick and frame buildings are destroyed. Large landslides are common. Water is thrown out of rivers and canals.

At the highest intensity level, XII (12), nearly all buildings are destroyed and the ground cracks in many places.

A seismograph is an instrument for recording vibrations caused by an earthquake. Older seismographs, like this one, used a suspended pen to record any jiggles on a slowly moving strip of paper. The resulting record is called a seismogram. Today, seismographs are hooked up directly to computers.

A Chinese scientist named Chang Heng designed the first seismometer (earthquake-measuring instrument) nearly 2000 years ago. The bronze "dragon jar" stood taller than a person and contained a heavy pendulum. When tremors shook the ground, the pendulum moved, causing one of eight dragons on the jar to drop its ball into the mouth of a toad below.

DISASTER DATA

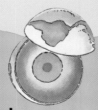

Every year, over 3 million minor earthquakes (with magnitudes below 5) vibrate our planet. About 800 moderate (5 to 5.9) and 120 strong (6 to 6.9) tremors jolt countries around the world. Major earthquakes (7 to 7.9) occur about eighteen times a year. What about magnitude 8 and beyond? Fortunately, these great quakes rock the ground, on average, only once a year.

Quake Shakes
FRISCO

San Francisco's baseball fans were thrilled. On October 17, 1989, their home team was ready to play the third game of the World Series. About 62 000 people packed Candlestick Park stadium and the game was about to begin when suddenly everything began to rock.

"Oh my God, we're having an earthquake," gasped the announcer. When the shaking stopped fifteen seconds later, everyone in the stadium was fine. They cheered wildly. They didn't realize that other parts of the city had not fared so well.

Several older homes in the Marina District toppled. Some caught fire. Most residents managed to escape, but a few were trapped in the wreckage. Fire crews quickly took command of the situation and in three hours the fires were out. Experts explained that the Marina District suffered more damage than other areas because its soft soil had turned soupy during the shaking.

San Francisco firefighters battle flames after the 1989 quake. Leaking gas pipes and downed electrical wires often trigger fires after a major earthquake. This blaze was brought under control within three hours. Fires following an earlier 1906 earthquake burned for four days.

In this aerial photo, the San Andreas Fault appears as a dark gash beside the highway. Along the fault, the Pacific plate drifts northward, sideswiping the North American plate. When the two plates jerk past each other, earthquakes shake San Francisco and southern California.

Even worse was the collapse of the multi-level Cypress Freeway. Emergency crews struggled to reach survivors on the severed upper deck, all the time aware that earthquake aftershocks (small earthquakes) could knock down the damaged structure. While they managed to pull some people from their crushed cars, dozens of others died.

A statue of scientist Louis Agassiz dove headfirst off a ledge during the strong earthquake that tossed San Francisco in 1906. Within minutes of the main shock, fires broke out. Soon, whole areas of the city were ablaze. In all, about 28 000 buildings were destroyed. An estimated 3000 people were killed.

A car is crushed under the third story of an apartment building in the Marina District of San Francisco. Lower levels of the building have collapsed and sunk into the ground. Damage was greatest in this part of the city because its soft soil turned mushy during the 1989 earthquake.

SWALLOWED ALIVE!

About 300 years ago, Port Royal, Jamaica, was called "The Wickedest City in the World." Its streets bustled with swaggering pirates and hard-hearted slave traders. By 1692, residents of the major port had witnessed plenty of wild goings-on. Still, no one was prepared for the coming catastrophe.

That year, just before noon on June 7, a violent earthquake shook Port Royal. People tried to run, but many found they couldn't move. Liquefaction turned Port Royal's sandy soil into mush. With every step, the panicked people plunged deeper and deeper into the quicksand. Some sank to their waists. Others were trapped with only their heads exposed. But most were swallowed completely.

People, buildings, trees and animals plunged into the watery ground. A few fortunate residents were spit back out and lived to tell their strange tale. An eyewitness reported, "Some were swallowed quite down, and cast up again by great Quantities of Water; others went down and were never more seen."

A 1692 newspaper illustrates the horrors of the Port Royal earthquake. Buildings collapse. A church tower crashes down. Many people disappear into cracks in the quicksand. Dogs sniff the heads of those buried up to their necks. A circle of citizens pray while others are washed out to sea.

Near the shore, whole streets sank as the soil below them flowed away. By the time the earthquake ended, two-thirds of the town had vanished beneath the waves. About 2500 people had perished. "The Wickedest City in the World" had weirdly disappeared.

Divers inspect the underwater ruins of Port Royal. Two-thirds of the city sank into the sea during the devastating earthquake of 1692. As one observer wrote, "Once brave Streets of stately houses [are] now Habitations for Fish."

DISASTER DATA

Earthquakes cause their greatest destruction in places where the soil is loose or sandy. A strong tremor shakes apart the individual grains in such soil, turning solid ground into a soft, wet slush. This process, called liquefaction, tilted buildings in San Francisco's Marina District and the Japanese port of Kobe. It also produced the quicksand that swallowed Port Royal. Once the shaking stops, the ground re-hardens but the damage has already been done.

Killer Waves

When earthquakes strike on dry land, they rattle dishes, shatter windows and knock down buildings. But when quakes happen underwater, they create strange hazards all their own — giant ocean waves called tsunamis.

Seconds after this photo was taken, the man on the pier was swept away. He was one of 159 people killed by a tsunami that destroyed the waterfront of Hilo, Hawaii, in 1946. The giant wave began when an earthquake shook the sea floor near the Aleutian Islands of Alaska.

DISASTER DATA

• The earth-shaking eruption of the Krakatoa volcano in 1883 flooded surrounding Indonesian islands and took the lives of 36 000 people.
• The largest tsunami on record hit the Ryūkyū Islands near Japan in 1971. It was nearly as high as a nine-story building.
• In the years between 1990 and 2000, ten great tsunamis caused the deaths of over 4000 people.
• Millions of sea turtles in Nicaragua were killed when a large tsunami washed them from their breeding grounds in 1992.

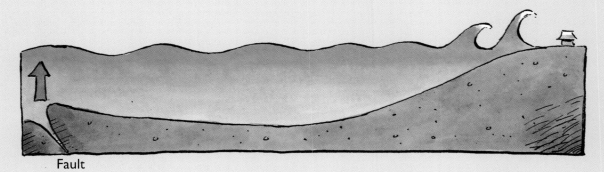

Fault

A tsunami is set off when an undersea quake raises the water above it. The tsunami is barely visible as it crosses the ocean, but rises higher and higher as it reaches the shore.

Tsunami is the Japanese word for "harbor wave." As their name implies, tsunamis are most deadly when they surge into a harbor or smash against an unprotected coastline.

Usually, each tsunami is made of a series of several huge waves. These watery monsters can be produced by underwater volcanoes and landslides. They can even be created when a meteorite hits the ocean. But, most often, tsunamis are set off by the sudden jolt of an undersea earthquake.

In deep water, a tsunami races invisibly, raising the surface in long, gentle slopes. Although it travels across the ocean at jet plane speeds of up to 700 km/hr (450 mph), a tsunami begins to reveal its terrible power only when it nears the shore.

The tsunami slows down as it reaches shallower water. Its waves rise into towering peaks, forming walls of water that can be 20 m (65 ft.) high or more.

When the tsunami hits the shore, people, buildings, ships and forests can all be swept away. Powerful tsunamis last much longer than wind-driven waves. They bounce back and forth across the ocean, often destroying places far from the spot where they began.

These before and after photos of a building show the devastating effects of a tsunami that struck Papua, New Guinea's north coast on July 17, 1998. A wall of water 4 m (12 ft.) high slammed against the shore, followed by another wave 15 m (46 ft.) high. Within minutes, several villages were flattened. Hundreds of people were swept out to sea. A magnitude 7.1 earthquake deep below the ocean floor had created the deadly tsunami.

Like a team of doctors swarming over a giant patient, scientists are working hard to understand the Earth. Seismologists use high-tech instruments to take its temperature, monitor its trembling and probe its depths.

Geologists dig into the ground to find clues about earthquakes long ago. What was the average length of time between tremors? How long ago was the last big shake? By searching through layers of rock and soil, geologists can piece together an area's seismic

QUAKE QUEST

history. Scientists also want to know what's happening right now. They measure ground movement by bouncing laser beams off mountains. Tiltmeters track changes in the slope of the land. Creepmeters check for slow, steady movement along fault lines. With the Global Positioning System, or GPS, seismologists use signals reflected from space satellites to detect land motion. If the ground shifts, they know that stress is building within the rock.

Understanding an area's past and present helps seismologists predict its future. They can warn if a site is too dangerous for building and help city officials set up emergency plans. But, because earthquakes are such complicated events, quake prediction is not precise. Scientists can estimate the chances of a major tremor in the next decade or century, but they're still stumped by one big question — *exactly* when will the next quake happen?

A geologist (a scientist who studies the Earth) checks soil layers in a trench dug across the San Andreas Fault in California. By figuring out the age of disrupted layers, geologists have discovered that a great earthquake shook the San Francisco area about 400 years ago.

Global Positioning System (GPS) satellites bounce signals back to high-tech equipment on the ground. They help seismologists make precise measurements and detect the tiny land movements that may lead to an earthquake.

东 北 虎
DONG BEI HU

On July 18, 1969, this tiger and other zoo animals in Tianjin, China, started to act strangely. Later in the day, a 7.4 magnitude earthquake shook the area. Although many people have observed that dogs bark wildly, cats howl and rats scurry around just before a major tremor, animal behavior has seldom been used successfully to predict an earthquake.

YOU TRY IT

Find out about the latest earthquakes happening around the world by visiting this site on the Internet:
http://neic.usgs.gov/neis/current/world.html

Preparing to SURVIVE

Japanese children practice earthquake safety by ducking under their desks during a school drill. They know that falling objects are the biggest danger during a quake.

People can't stop earthquakes from happening, but they can reduce the damage they cause. Well-equipped emergency teams can rescue people from fallen buildings. Firefighters and hospital workers learn to deal with these crises.

A rescue worker and her dog help search for survivors of the 1985 earthquake in Mexico City. International rescue teams and their trained "sniffer dogs" fly quickly to the site of a major disaster. Because damaged buildings can easily collapse during an aftershock, rescuers risk their own lives when they attempt to save others.

DISASTER DATA

Earthquake survivors are often trapped in hollow spaces under crumpled walls and floors. Rescuers must get to them quickly, in case they are injured or aftershocks lead to further collapse. Specially trained dogs, heat-sensing cameras and portable vibration detectors help find anyone who is still alive. Then, rescuers work with chain saws, pickaxes and their bare hands to reach the victims.

Individuals can also prepare for earthquakes. If you live in or visit an earthquake-prone area, here are some steps you and your family can take to keep yourselves safe.

• Practice taking cover. You will be safest under a heavy table or desk, in a hallway or in the corner of a room. Stay away from windows, mirrors and kitchen cupboards.

• Check for objects that could fall on you during a quake. Keep heavy things on lower shelves.

• Place beds away from windows and heavy pictures. Close the curtains or blinds while you are sleeping.

• Keep sturdy shoes and a flashlight handy.

• Plan where to meet after a quake. Make sure everyone in the family has an out-of-town phone number to call in case you are separated.

Two boys wash up at an emergency station after the 1994 earthquake in Northridge, California. Germs spread quickly when a disaster breaks water and sewer lines and forces people left homeless into crowded spaces.

• Pack an emergency kit with non-perishable food, water, first-aid supplies, a battery-operated radio, coins for phone calls and a flashlight.

Building for the BIG ONE

In one country, a magnitude 6 earthquake shatters buildings and shakes whole towns to the ground. Elsewhere, a similar magnitude quake causes only minor damage. Why the difference? An earthquake's effects depend on what local buildings are made of and how they're put together.

Some countries, such as Japan, Canada and the United States, have strict regulations about construction in earthquake-prone areas. New houses, apartments, office towers and bridges must be designed to withstand at least a moderate shaking.

The Transamerica Pyramid is one of San Francisco's most famous landmarks. The 48-story building was designed with a wide base and tapering top to make it more stable. During the 1989 earthquake, the top floor of the Pyramid swayed over 30 cm (1 ft.), but no one was injured and the building was not damaged.

High-strength steel and reinforced concrete help make structures both strong and flexible. Adding cross-bracing to the building and anchoring its foundation help reduce damaging movement during a quake. Some buildings have been placed on rubber pads that absorb earthquake energy in the same way that the soles of your running shoes absorb the shock of your steps.

Engineers are working on new ways to make buildings earthquake-proof. Advanced computer programs help them figure out the stresses that act on a building during a tremor. Model buildings let them see what holds up best under severe shaking. Instead of stiff, brittle structures, the new designs allow for some movement. The building or bridge should sway — but not too much.

An engineer watches as a model adobe house rocks and sways on a special "shake table." Cracks appear where the house will eventually fall apart. By testing models, engineers improve the seismic safety of full-scale buildings.

Some new buildings, called smart buildings, have built-in sensors to detect earthquake activity. When the sensors pick up ground movement, they trigger computer-controlled devices in the building's framework. These devices work to lessen the earthquake's effect. One experimental building in Tokyo, Japan, for instance, has large weights in its upper levels. These swing in the opposite direction to an incoming shock wave, reducing the building's vibrations.

You Try It

Find out how buildings are braced for an earthquake. Mix two packages of Jell-O in a 23 cm by 33 cm (9 in. by 13 in.) baking pan. When the Jell-O sets, break dry spaghetti into 12 pieces, each 15 cm (6 in.) long. Build a cube using miniature marshmallows to connect the spaghetti pieces at right angles. Place your structure on the Jell-O and jiggle the pan to model an earthquake. What happens? Now rebuild the structure using longer pieces of spaghetti to join the corners of each wall diagonally. Test your cross-braced building. Will it stand up to a quake?

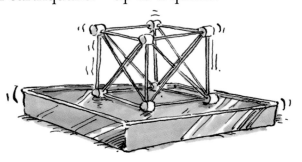

Life on a RESTLESS PLANET

Five years after the terrible earthquake of 1995, life was almost back to normal in the city of Kobe. The rebuilt harbor welcomed ocean-going cruise ships and freighters. Stores and schools were now open in strong new structures. Earthquake victims had all been moved from temporary, mobile homes to permanent housing.

Earthquakes are a sign of Nature's power. They shape the land and remind us that our planet is constantly changing. Though major quakes cause horrible damage, people are finding better ways to protect themselves. Every day, scientists learn more about why, where and when earthquakes happen. Engineers design earthquake-resistant buildings, and city

Japanese schoolchildren wear padded hoods during an earthquake drill. During a real quake, the hoods would help protect them from falling debris.

planners prepare for major emergencies. Everyone is working toward one goal — to make people safer when the Earth shudders and shakes.

Glossary

Continent: one of seven major landmasses on Earth

Core: the center portion of the Earth

Creepmeter: an instrument for measuring slow ground movement

Crust: the solid outer layer of the Earth

Earthquake: a sudden shaking of the ground caused when rock breaks

Epicenter: the place on Earth's surface directly above an earthquake's focus

Focus: the place underground where breaking rock starts an earthquake

Geologist: a scientist who studies the Earth

Geyser: a fountain of hot water and steam that spurts up into the air. The water is heated inside the Earth

Liquefaction: the process in which solid ground turns to mush during an earthquake

Magnitude: a measure of an earthquake's strength

Mantle: the middle layer of Earth's interior between the core and the crust

Richter scale: a ranking of earthquake power, from zero to nine or more

Rift: a split between tectonic plates that are moving apart

Seismograph: an instrument for recording ground vibrations during an earthquake

Seismologist: a scientist who studies earthquakes

Seismometer: an instrument for measuring an earthquake's intensity and location

Tectonic plates: slabs of Earth's crust and upper mantle layer

Tiltmeter: an instrument for measuring changes in ground slope

Tsunami: a series of huge ocean waves, usually set off by an undersea volcano or earthquake

Volcano: any place where melted rock emerges through Earth's crust

Index